make me

soups

MURDOCH BOOKS

HIGH LIFE HIGHLAND

3800 12 0076776 6	
Askews & Holts	Oct-2012
641.813	£6.99

Contents

Introduction

Simple, versatile and always satisfying, soups have the ability to warm the soul no matter how cold it is outside. What could be more comforting than a rustic minestrone, more energising than a spicy tom yum goong or more satisfying than a classic chicken noodle soup?

Make Me Soups has a recipe for any occasion or culinary craving—visit Morocco with a bowl of hearty harira; travel to south-east Asia with every spoonful of a spicy Vietnamese beef & pork noodle soup; taste winter in Europe with a goulash soup with herb dumplings; or even go south of the border with a Mexican cream of corn soup.

While the soups are definitely the star, a simple accompaniment can take a soup to new heights. At the back of this book you will find a basics section packed with simple yet clever ideas to sprinkle over, stir though and dip into your soups. Choose them to customise your soups and give them an extra dimension depending on the occasion.

Whether you're searching for a classic soup, a complete meal in a bowl, a lighter-style soup or one that will take very little time or effort, *Make Me Soups* will be the book to visit regularly for simple yet inspirational recipes.

Classics

Roasted tomato soup

Preparation time: 20 minutes
Cooking time: 1 hour 15 minutes
Serves: 4

1.5 kg (3 lb 5 oz) ripe tomatoes, cores removed, halved
2 brown onions, unpeeled, halved
1 whole garlic bulb
2 tablespoons olive oil
sea salt flakes, to sprinkle
1 litre (35 fl oz/4 cups) good-quality chicken stock
sugar, to taste
½ cup basil leaves, to serve
shaved parmesan cheese, to serve

1 Preheat oven to 180°C (350°F/Gas 4). Put the tomato halves, onion halves and garlic in a roasting tin, drizzle with the olive oil and sprinkle with sea salt. Roast for 45–55 minutes or until soft. Set aside for 10 minutes or until cool enough to handle.

2 Remove the outer skin from the onion halves, put in a food processor and pulse until roughly chopped. Transfer the onion to a large saucepan. Cut off the root end of the garlic and squeeze out the roasted garlic pulp. Put the garlic in a food processor with half the roasted tomatoes and process until puréed. Add to the saucepan with the remaining roasted tomatoes and the stock.

3 Place the saucepan over high heat and bring to the boil. Reduce the heat to low and simmer for 15 minutes or until the tomatoes partially break down.

4 Season with salt and a little sugar (the sugar is to round out the flavours—how much you need will depend upon the ripeness of the tomatoes). Serve immediately, topped with the basil and parmesan.

Chicken laksa

Preparation time: 30 minutes
Cooking time: 40 minutes
Serves: 4–6

1½ tablespoons coriander seeds
1 tablespoon cumin seeds
1 teaspoon ground turmeric
3 teaspoons shrimp paste
1 brown onion, roughly chopped
1 tablespoon roughly chopped ginger
3 garlic cloves
3 lemongrass stems, white part only, sliced
6 macadamia nuts
4–6 fresh small red chillies
1 litre (35 fl oz/4 cups) good-quality
  chicken stock
60 ml (2 fl oz/¼ cup) peanut oil
400 g (14 oz) skinless chicken thigh fillets,
  trimmed, cut into 2 cm (¾ in) pieces

750 ml (26 fl oz/3 cups) coconut milk
4 kaffir lime leaves
2½ tablespoons freshly squeezed
  lime juice
2 tablespoons fish sauce
2 tablespoons grated palm sugar
  (jaggery) or soft brown sugar
250 g (9 oz) dried rice vermicelli
115 g (4 oz/1 cup) bean sprouts, trimmed
4 fried tofu puffs, cut into strips
¼ cup Vietnamese mint leaves
½ cup coriander (cilantro) leaves
lime wedges, to serve

1 Toast the coriander and cumin seeds in a small frying pan over medium heat for 1–2 minutes or until aromatic, tossing the pan constantly to prevent them from burning. Use a mortar and pestle or a spice grinder to grind finely.
2 Preheat grill (broiler) to high. Wrap the shrimp paste in a small piece of foil and place under preheated grill for 2 minutes or until aromatic, turning halfway through cooking.
3 Put all the spices, shrimp paste, onion, ginger, garlic, lemongrass, macadamia nuts and chillies in a food processor or blender. Add 125 ml (4 fl oz/½ cup) of the stock and blend to a paste.
4 Heat the peanut oil in a wok or large saucepan over low heat and gently cook the paste for 3–5 minutes, stirring constantly to prevent it burning or sticking to the base of the

pan. Add the remaining stock and bring to the boil over high heat. Reduce the heat to medium and simmer for 15 minutes or until reduced slightly.
5 Add the chicken and simmer for 4–5 minutes. Add the coconut milk, lime leaves, lime juice, fish sauce and palm sugar and simmer for 5 minutes over medium–low heat. (Do not boil or cover with a lid, as the coconut milk will split.)
6 Meanwhile, put the vermicelli in a large heatproof bowl, cover with boiling water and soak for 6–7 minutes or until soft. Drain and divide among large serving bowls with the bean sprouts. Ladle the hot soup over the vermicelli and top with the tofu strips and mint and coriander leaves. Serve immediately with lime wedges.

Cream of spinach soup

Preparation time: 15 minutes
Cooking time: 25 minutes
Serves: 4

3–4 bunches (about 750 g/1 lb 10 oz)
  English spinach, trimmed
1 tablespoon olive oil
1 brown onion, chopped
1 garlic clove, chopped
1 large (about 250 g/9 oz) potato,
  peeled, cut into 1 cm (½ in) dice
1.25 litres (44 fl oz/5 cups) good-quality
  salt-reduced chicken or vegetable stock
750 ml (26 fl oz/3 cups) pouring
  (whipping) cream
70 g (2½ oz/¾ cup) coarsely grated
  parmesan cheese

> **TIP:** To keep the spinach bright green, only cook it until it just wilts and then blend it as soon as possible.

1 Pick the leaves from the spinach and wash thoroughly. (You will need about 400 g/14 oz leaves.) Roughly chop the leaves and set aside.

2 Put the olive oil, onion and garlic in a large saucepan over medium–low heat and cook for 5 minutes, stirring occasionally, or until soft.

3 Add the potato and stock, increase the heat to high and bring to the boil. Reduce the heat to low and simmer for 15 minutes or until the potato is soft.

4 Increase the heat to medium, add half the cream and bring to a simmer. Stir through the chopped spinach and cook for 1 minute or until just wilted. Stir through the remaining cream and half the parmesan (this will cool the soup down slightly so you can blend it immediately).

5 Transfer the soup in batches to a food processor or blender and process until the spinach is finely chopped. Return the soup to the saucepan and reheat over medium heat. Season with salt. Serve sprinkled with the remaining parmesan.

French onion soup

Preparation time: 20 minutes
Cooking time: 1 hour 30 minutes
Serves: 6 as a starter

60 g (2¼ oz) butter
6 (about 1.2 kg/2 lb 10 oz) brown onions,
 thinly sliced into rings
35 g (1¼ oz/¼ cup) plain flour
1 teaspoon sugar
2 litres (70 fl oz/8 cups) good-quality
 salt-reduced vegetable stock
250 ml (9 fl oz/1 cup) water
12 x 1 cm (½ in) baguette slices
65 g (2½ oz/⅔ cup, loosely packed) coarsely
 grated gruyère or cheddar cheese

1 Melt the butter in a large saucepan. Add the onion and cook over low heat for 20 minutes or until tender and lightly golden. Increase the heat to medium. Add the flour and sugar and stir for 1–2 minutes or until the flour becomes golden.

2 Add the stock and water and bring to a simmer. Cover and cook over low heat for 1 hour, stirring occasionally. Season with salt and freshly ground black pepper.

3 Meanwhile, preheat oven to 180°C (350°F/Gas 4). Bake the baguette slices for 10 minutes, turning once, until dry and golden. Preheat grill (broiler) to high. Top each baguette slice with some of the grated cheese and place under preheated grill for 2 minutes or until the cheese melts.

4 Serve the soup topped with the cheesy croutons.

Creamy cauliflower soup

Preparation time: 10 minutes
Cooking time: 30 minutes
Serves: 4

½ large cauliflower
2½ tablespoons olive oil
1 leek, pale section only, chopped
1.125 litres (39 fl oz/4½ cups) good-quality chicken
  or vegetable stock
300 ml (10½ fl oz) pouring (whipping) cream
100 g (3½ oz/1 cup, loosely packed) coarsely grated
  vintage cheddar cheese, or 40 g (1½ oz) firm
  blue cheese, crumbled
cayenne pepper, to serve

1 Trim the florets from the cauliflower and cut into rough 2.5 cm (1 in) pieces. (You will need about 800 g/1 lb 12 oz of trimmed cauliflower.)

2 Put the olive oil, leek and cauliflower in a large saucepan over medium–low heat and cook for 10 minutes, stirring occasionally, or until the leek is soft.

3 Add the stock, increase the heat to high and bring to the boil. Reduce the heat to low and simmer for 15 minutes or until the cauliflower is tender. Remove from the heat and stir in the cream and cheese.

4 Cool slightly then transfer the soup in batches to a food processor or blender and process until smooth. Return the soup to the saucepan and reheat over medium heat. Season with salt and serve sprinkled with cayenne pepper.

Red gazpacho

Preparation time: 40 minutes (+ 2 hours chilling time)
Cooking time: nil
Serves: 4

1 kg (2 lb 4 oz) vine-ripened tomatoes
2 thick slices (about 70 g/2½ oz) day-old white
   Italian bread, crusts removed, broken into pieces
1 red capsicum (pepper), seeded, roughly chopped
2 garlic cloves, chopped
1 fresh small green chilli (optional), chopped
1 teaspoon sugar
2 tablespoons red wine vinegar
2 tablespoons extra virgin olive oil
freshly ground white pepper, to taste
8 ice cubes, to serve

Garnish
½ Lebanese (short) cucumber, seeded, finely diced
½ red capsicum (pepper), seeded, finely diced
½ green capsicum (pepper), seeded, finely diced
½ red onion, finely diced
½ ripe tomato, diced

1 Score a cross in the base of the tomatoes. Put the tomatoes in a medium heatproof bowl and cover with boiling water. Leave for 30 seconds, then transfer to cold water and peel the skin away from the cross. Cut the tomatoes in half, scoop out the seeds and roughly chop the flesh.
2 Soak the bread in cold water for 5 minutes, then squeeze out any excess liquid. Put the bread in a food processor with the tomato, capsicum, garlic, chilli, if using, sugar and vinegar, and process until smooth.
3 With the motor running, add the olive oil to make a smooth, creamy mixture. Season to taste with salt and white pepper. Refrigerate for at least 2 hours or until well chilled. Add a little extra vinegar, if desired.
4 For the garnish, mix all the ingredients in a bowl.
5 To serve, ladle the soup into serving bowls, add 2 ice cubes to each and scatter with the garnish.

Pumpkin soup with harissa

Preparation time: 20 minutes
Cooking time: 20 minutes
Serves: 4–6

2.5 kg (5 lb 8 oz) pumpkin (winter squash)
750 ml (26 fl oz/3 cups) good-quality
  vegetable stock
750 ml (26 fl oz/3 cups) milk
sugar, to taste

Harissa
125 g (4½ oz) fresh long red chillies
2 teaspoons caraway seeds
2 teaspoons coriander seeds
1 teaspoon cumin seeds
2 large garlic cloves
2 teaspoons dried mint
60 ml (2 fl oz/¼ cup) extra virgin olive oil

1 Remove the skin, seeds and fibre from the pumpkin and cut into 5–6 cm (2–2½ in) chunks. Put the pumpkin in a large saucepan with the stock and milk. Bring to the boil and then simmer for 15 minutes or until tender.

2 Meanwhile, to make the harissa, wear disposable gloves to remove the stems of the chillies, split them in half lengthways, remove the seeds and soften the flesh in hot water for 5 minutes. Toast the caraway, coriander and cumin seeds in a frying pan for 1–2 minutes or until aromatic. Drain the chillies and put in a food processor. Add the seeds, garlic, mint and 1 teaspoon of salt to the processor and process, slowly adding the olive oil, until a smooth, thick paste forms.

3 Cool the soup slightly then transfer in batches to a food processor and process until smooth. Return the soup to a clean saucepan and season to taste with a little sugar and freshly ground black pepper. Gently reheat.

4 Serve the soup topped with a spoonful of harissa. Serve any remaining harissa separately.

Chinese chicken noodle soup

Preparation time: 35 minutes
Cooking time: 2 hours 20 minutes
Serves: 4–6

2 kg (4 lb 8 oz) chicken wings
1 brown onion, chopped
1 carrot, chopped
1 celery stalk, chopped
1 cinnamon stick
1 star anise
1½ tablespoons very finely shredded ginger
1 tablespoon light soy sauce
2½ tablespoons dry sherry
1.5 litres (52 fl oz/6 cups) water
600 g (1 lb 5 oz) skinless chicken thigh fillets,
    trimmed, thinly sliced
3 heads (about 400 g/14 oz) choy sum or bok choy (pak choy),
    trimmed, very thinly sliced widthways
200 g (7 oz) shiitake mushrooms, stems trimmed, sliced
400 g (14 oz) fresh Singapore-style (thin) egg noodles
1 spring onion (scallion), trimmed, diagonally
    sliced, to serve
sesame oil (optional), to serve
sliced fresh long red chilli (optional), to serve

1 Combine the chicken wings, onion, carrot, celery, cinnamon stick, star anise, ginger, soy sauce and sherry in a large saucepan. Add the water, then bring to the boil over medium heat, skimming any scum that rises to the surface. Reduce the heat to low, then cook for 2 hours, skimming the surface occasionally. Strain the stock, discarding the solids and removing any fat from the surface.
2 Return the stock to the pan. Add the chicken thighs and slowly bring to a gentle simmer. Add the choy sum or bok choy, mushrooms and noodles and stir to combine. Cook for another 4–5 minutes or until the chicken, vegetables and noodles are tender.
3 Season to taste with salt and freshly ground black pepper. Serve immediately, topped with the spring onion and sesame oil and chilli, if using.

Leek & potato soup

Preparation time: 15 minutes
Cooking time: 25 minutes
Serves: 4

50 g (1¾ oz) butter
2 leeks, pale section only, chopped
1 celery stalk, thinly sliced
1 fresh bay leaf
500 g (1 lb 2 oz) potatoes (see tip),
   peeled, chopped
750 ml (26 fl oz/3 cups) water
2 tablespoons finely snipped chives, to serve

1 Melt the butter in a large saucepan over medium heat. Add the leek, celery and bay leaf. Cook, stirring, for 2 minutes or until the leek starts to soften. Reduce the heat to low and cook, covered, for 5 minutes or until the vegetables are soft.

2 Add the potato and water. Season with salt and freshly ground black pepper and stir well. Bring to the boil over high heat. Reduce the heat to low and simmer, covered, for 12 minutes or until the vegetables are tender. Discard the bay leaf.

3 Cool slightly then transfer the soup in batches to a food processor or blender and process until smooth. Strain through a fine sieve, pressing down with the back of a ladle (see tip). Return the soup to the saucepan and reheat over medium heat. Serve sprinkled with the chives.

TIPS: Floury potatoes are better for this kind of soup. Look out for any potatoes recommended for mash, such as King Edward or golden delight potatoes.

It is not absolutely necessary to strain the soup but the final result will be much silkier if you do.

Tom yum goong

Preparation time: 25 minutes
Cooking time: 45 minutes
Serves: 4–6

1 tablespoon peanut oil
500 g (1 lb 2 oz) raw prawns (shrimp), peeled, deveined,
  tails left intact, shells and heads reserved
2 tablespoons red curry paste
2 teaspoons ground turmeric
2 litres (70 fl oz/8 cups) water
2 tablespoons tamarind concentrate (see tip)
6 kaffir lime leaves, shredded
2 tablespoons fish sauce
2 tablespoons freshly squeezed lime juice
2 teaspoons soft brown sugar
1 cup coriander (cilantro) leaves, to serve
1 bird's eye chilli (optional), chopped, to serve

TIP: Tamarind concentrate is available from the Asian section of selected supermarkets or from Asian grocery stores.

1 Heat the peanut oil in a large saucepan, add the prawn shells and heads to the pan and cook for 10 minutes over high heat, stirring often, until the shells and heads are deep orange in colour.
2 Add the curry paste and turmeric to the pan and cook over medium heat for 1 minute or until aromatic. Add 250 ml (9 fl oz/1 cup) of the water and bring to the boil. Boil for 5 minutes or until the liquid has reduced slightly. Add the remaining water and simmer for 20 minutes. Strain the stock, discarding the prawn heads and shells.
3 Return the strained stock to the pan. Add the tamarind concentrate and lime leaves, bring to the boil and cook for 2 minutes. Add the prawns to the pan and simmer for 3–5 minutes or until the prawns turn pink and are just cooked through. Add the fish sauce, lime juice and sugar and stir to combine. Taste and adjust seasoning if necessary. Serve immediately, scattered with the coriander and the chilli, if using.

Mixed vegetable soup

Preparation time: 20 minutes
Cooking time: 45 minutes
Serves: 4–6

40 g (1½ oz) butter
1 leek, pale section only, thinly sliced
2 carrots, peeled, chopped
1 celery stalk, chopped
400 g (14 oz) Sebago potatoes, peeled, chopped
400 g (14 oz) sweet potato, peeled, chopped
2 teaspoons sweet paprika
2 teaspoons ground fennel seeds
2 garlic cloves, chopped
2 tablespoons tomato paste (concentrated purée)
1 litre (35 fl oz/4 cups) good-quality chicken stock
500 ml (17 fl oz/2 cups) water
125 ml (4 fl oz/½ cup) milk
grated parmesan cheese, to serve
finely snipped chives, to serve

1 Melt the butter in a large saucepan over medium heat. Add the leek, carrot, celery, potato and sweet potato. Cook, stirring, for 10 minutes or until the vegetables start to soften. Add the spices and garlic and cook, stirring, for 1 minute. Add the tomato paste and cook, stirring, for 1 minute.
2 Add the stock and water. Bring to the boil, then reduce the heat to low and simmer, uncovered, for 30 minutes or until the vegetables are very soft.
3 Cool slightly then transfer the soup in batches to a food processor and process until smooth. Return the soup to the saucepan and add the milk. Cook, stirring, for 3 minutes or until heated through (do not bring to the boil). Season with salt and freshly ground black pepper to taste.
4 Serve sprinkled with the parmesan and chives.

Tuscan bread soup

Preparation time: 20 minutes
Cooking time: 55 minutes
Serves: 4

1.5 kg (3 lb 5 oz) ripe tomatoes, halved
60 ml (2 fl oz/¼ cup) olive oil
1 large brown onion, chopped
4 basil leaves
2 garlic cloves, crushed
500 ml (17 fl oz/2 cups) good-quality chicken stock
1 teaspoon caster sugar
150 g (5½ oz) stale ciabatta bread, chopped
2 tablespoons red wine vinegar
250 ml (9 fl oz/1 cup) water
extra virgin olive oil, to serve
crisp basil leaves (see page 117), shredded, to serve

1 Preheat oven to 180°C (350°F/Gas 4). Place the tomatoes cut side up on a baking tray lined with non-stick baking paper. Season to taste with salt and freshly ground black pepper. Roast for 30 minutes or until soft.

2 Heat the olive oil in a large saucepan over medium heat. Add the onion and basil leaves. Cook, stirring, for 5 minutes, or until the onion is soft. Add the garlic and cook, stirring, for 1 minute. Add the stock, sugar, roasted tomatoes and any cooking juices. Simmer, uncovered, for 15 minutes.

3 Meanwhile, combine the bread, vinegar and water in a medium bowl. Stand for 10 minutes or until soft. Stir into the soup.

4 Cool slightly then transfer the soup in batches to a food processor and process until smooth. Return the soup to the saucepan and bring to a simmer. Season to taste with salt and freshly ground black pepper. Serve drizzled with the olive oil and sprinkled with the crisp basil.

Chinese chicken & corn soup

Preparation time: 20 minutes
Cooking time: 20 minutes
Serves: 4

750 ml (26 fl oz/3 cups) good-quality
  chicken stock
2 x 200 g (7 oz) skinless chicken breast
  fillets, trimmed, cut in half lengthways
1 tablespoon vegetable oil
4 spring onions (scallions), thinly sliced,
  white and green parts separated
1 garlic clove, crushed
2 teaspoons finely grated fresh ginger
250 ml (9 fl oz/1 cup) water
3–4 corn cobs (see tip), kernels removed
420 g (15 oz) tin creamed corn
2 tablespoons light soy sauce
1 tablespoon Chinese rice wine
1 tablespoon cornflour (cornstarch)
2 teaspoons sesame oil

TIP: You will need about 400 g (14 oz/2 cups) of corn kernels for this recipe.

1 Bring the stock to simmering point in a small saucepan. Add the chicken and simmer, covered, for 5 minutes. Remove the chicken with a slotted spoon and allow to rest for 10 minutes. Strain the stock and set aside. Finely shred the meat with two forks.

2 Heat a wok over medium–high heat, add the vegetable oil and swirl to coat the side of the wok. Add the white part of the spring onion, the garlic and ginger and stir-fry for 30 seconds. Add the stock, water, corn kernels, creamed corn, soy sauce and rice wine. Stir until the soup comes to the boil. Reduce the heat and simmer for 10 minutes.

3 Meanwhile, stir the cornflour, sesame oil and 1 tablespoon of water together in a small bowl until smooth. Add a little of the hot stock, stir together, then pour this mixture into the soup. Bring to simmering point, stirring constantly for 3–4 minutes, or until slightly thickened. Add the chicken meat and heat through. Season to taste with salt and freshly ground black pepper. Serve immediately, topped with the spring onion greens.

Meal in a bowl

Easy bouillabaisse

Preparation time: 25 minutes
Cooking time: 40 minutes
Serves: 4

125 ml (4 fl oz/½ cup) warm water
1 large pinch saffron threads
1 tablespoon olive oil
1 fennel bulb, thinly sliced, fronds reserved
2 garlic cloves, thinly sliced
1 fresh bay leaf
3 thyme sprigs
400 g (14 oz) tin chopped tomatoes
1.25 litres (44 fl oz/5 cups) good-quality
   chicken stock
500 g (1 lb 2 oz) skinless, boneless firm
   white fish fillets, cut into large chunks
500 g (1 lb 2 oz) raw king prawns (shrimp),
   peeled, deveined, tails left intact
500 g (1 lb 2 oz) mussels, scrubbed,
   debearded (see tip)

Garlic croutons
½ baguette, thinly sliced
2 tablespoons olive oil
1 garlic clove, halved

TIP: Prepare the mussels by scrubbing the shells and pulling out the hairy beards. Discard any that have broken shells, or ones that don't close when tapped on the bench. Rinse well.

1 Combine the water and saffron and set aside.

2 Meanwhile, heat the olive oil in a large saucepan over medium heat. Add the fennel and cook, stirring, for 10 minutes or until soft. Add the garlic, bay leaf and thyme. Cook, stirring, for 1 minute.

3 Add the saffron mixture, tomatoes and stock to the pan. Increase the heat to high. Bring to the boil, then reduce the heat and simmer for 20 minutes.

4 Meanwhile, for the garlic croutons, preheat the grill (broiler) to medium–high. Brush the bread slices on both sides with the oil, then rub the bread all over with the cut side of the garlic. Place on a baking tray under preheated grill for 1–2 minutes each side or until lightly golden.

5 Add the fish, prawns and mussels to the pan and cook over medium–low heat for 4–5 minutes, stirring occasionally, or until the fish is just tender and the mussels have opened. (Discard any unopened mussels.) Season to taste with salt and freshly ground black pepper. Serve immediately, topped with the fennel fronds and with the croutons on the side.

Harira

Preparation time: 20 minutes
Cooking time: 2 hours 20 minutes
Serves: 4

2 tablespoons olive oil
500 g (1 lb 2 oz) lamb shoulder steaks, trimmed,
  cut into small chunks
2 small brown onions, chopped
2 large garlic cloves, crushed
1½ teaspoons ground cumin
2 teaspoons paprika
½ teaspoon ground cloves
1 fresh bay leaf
2 tablespoons tomato paste (concentrated purée)
1 litre (35 fl oz/4 cups) good-quality beef stock
2 x 400 g (14 oz) tins chickpeas, rinsed, drained
800 g (1 lb 12 oz) tin chopped tomatoes
1 cup coriander (cilantro) leaves, finely chopped,
  plus extra leaves, to serve
small black olives, to serve
pitta bread, to serve

1 Heat the olive oil in a large saucepan or stockpot over medium–high heat and cook half the lamb, tossing occasionally, for 4–5 minutes or until browned. Remove from the pan and repeat with the remaining lamb. Reduce the heat to medium and cook the onion for 8 minutes or until soft. Add the garlic, spices and bay leaf and cook for 1 minute or until aromatic.

2 Return the lamb to the pan with the tomato paste and cook for 2 minutes, stirring constantly. Add the stock, stir well and bring to the boil.

3 Add the chickpeas, tomatoes and chopped coriander to the pan. Bring to the boil, reduce the heat and simmer for 2 hours, stirring occasionally, or until the lamb is very tender.

4 Season to taste with salt and freshly ground black pepper. Serve scattered with the coriander leaves, and accompanied by the olives and pitta bread.

Root vegetable soup

Preparation time: 10 minutes
Cooking time: 35 minutes
Serves: 4

2 tablespoons olive oil
1 leek, pale section only, chopped
2 garlic cloves, chopped
3 large carrots (about 650 g/1 lb 7 oz in total), peeled, cut into 2 cm (¾ in) chunks
2 parsnips (about 380 g/13½ oz in total), peeled, cut into 2 cm (¾ in) chunks
1 turnip (about 150 g/5½ oz), peeled, cut into 2 cm (¾ in) chunks
1.6 litres (55½ fl oz) good-quality chicken stock
2 tablespoons honey
1 tablespoon wholegrain mustard
crisp sage (see page 117) or finely snipped chives,
  and crusty bread, to serve

1 Put the olive oil and leek in a large saucepan over medium–low heat and cook for 8–10 minutes or until the leek is soft. Add the garlic and cook, stirring, for 1 minute.

2 Add the carrot, parsnip, turnip and stock, increase the heat to high and bring to the boil. Reduce the heat to low and simmer for 20 minutes or until the vegetables are tender. Stir through the honey.

3 Cool slightly then transfer the soup in batches to a food processor or blender and process until smooth. Return the soup to the saucepan and reheat over medium heat. Stir through the wholegrain mustard and season with salt. Serve topped with crisp sage or chives and accompanied by crusty bread.

Shanghai chicken & noodle soup

Preparation time: 15 minutes
Cooking time: 30–35 minutes
Serves: 4–6

5 cm (2 in) piece fresh ginger, peeled
2 litres (70 fl oz/8 cups) good-quality chicken stock
500 ml (17 fl oz/2 cups) water
1 star anise
600 g (1 lb 5 oz) skinless chicken breast fillets, trimmed
375 g (13 oz) Shanghai noodles
200 g (7 oz) asparagus, trimmed, cut into 3 cm (1¼ in) lengths
1½ tablespoons light soy sauce, plus extra (optional), to serve
1 tablespoon Chinese rice wine
½ teaspoon sugar
4 spring onions (scallions), thinly diagonally sliced
50 g (1¾ oz) watercress tips (optional)
¼ teaspoon sesame oil, to drizzle

1 Cut four thin slices from the ginger. Cut the remaining ginger into thin strips.
2 Pour the stock and water into a wok and bring to the boil over high heat. Reduce the heat to medium–low and add the star anise and ginger slices. Add the chicken, reduce the heat to low and poach gently for 15–20 minutes or until just cooked through. Remove the chicken with a slotted spoon and set aside to cool. Leave the stock in the wok.
3 Meanwhile, bring a large saucepan of water to the boil. Add the noodles and cook for 3 minutes or until almost tender. Drain and refresh under cold water. Set aside.
4 Cut the chicken across the grain into 5 mm (¼ in) slices.
5 Return the stock to the boil and add the asparagus, ginger strips, soy sauce, rice wine, sugar and ½ teaspoon of salt. Reduce the heat, add the noodles and simmer for 2 minutes. Return the chicken to the wok and cook for 1 minute, or until heated through.
6 Remove the noodles from the liquid with tongs and divide evenly among serving bowls. Divide the chicken, asparagus, spring onion and watercress, if using, among the bowls, then ladle the broth over. Drizzle with sesame oil and serve immediately, with extra soy sauce, if using.

ed bean & sausage soup

Preparation time: 20 minutes
Cooking time: 25 minutes
Serves: 6–8

100 ml (3½ fl oz) olive oil
2 leeks, pale section only, chopped
2 celery stalks, chopped
600 g (1 lb 5 oz) (about 8 thin) fresh Italian
  fennel-flavoured sausages
2 litres (70 fl oz/8 cups) good-quality chicken stock
2 dried bay leaves
400 g (14 oz) tin borlotti (cranberry) beans, rinsed, drained
400 g (14 oz) tin cannellini beans, rinsed, drained
400 g (14 oz) tin chickpeas, rinsed, drained
65 g (2½ oz/½ cup) macaroni (pasta elbows)
chopped flat-leaf (Italian) parsley, to serve
90 g (3¼ oz/⅓ cup) pesto (see page 118), to serve
80 g (2¾ oz/¾ cup) coarsely grated pecorino cheese, to serve

1 Heat the olive oil in a large saucepan over medium heat. Add the leek and celery and cook, stirring, for 6–7 minutes or until soft.

2 Meanwhile, remove the sausages from their casings, squeezing them out and breaking them into small portions. Add the sausage meat to the pan and cook, stirring occasionally, for 5 minutes or until it changes colour.

3 Add the stock and bay leaves to the pan, bring to a simmer then reduce the heat to low. Cook for 10 minutes or until the vegetables are very tender. Add the beans and chickpeas and bring to a simmer.

4 Meanwhile, cook the pasta in boiling salted water until al dente. Drain well. Add to the soup and bring back to a simmer. Season to taste with salt and freshly ground black pepper. Serve immediately, topped with the parsley, pesto and pecorino.

Chicken & chorizo soup with chickpeas

Preparation time: 20 minutes
Cooking time: 35 minutes
Serves: 4

125 ml (4 fl oz/½ cup) water
1 large pinch saffron threads
2 tablespoons olive oil
1 large brown onion, finely chopped
2 red capsicums (peppers), seeded, thinly sliced
1 chorizo (about 150 g/5½ oz), thinly sliced
2 garlic cloves, crushed
2 teaspoons smoked paprika
1 teaspoon sweet paprika
4 vine-ripened tomatoes, chopped
1 litre (35 fl oz/4 cups) good-quality chicken stock
300 g (10½ oz/2½ cups) shredded barbecued chicken
400 g (14 oz) tin chickpeas, rinsed, drained
2 tablespoons flat-leaf (Italian) parsley, finely chopped, to serve
toasted sourdough bread, to serve

1 Combine the water and saffron and set aside.

2 Heat the olive oil in a large saucepan over medium heat. Add the onion, capsicum and chorizo and cook, stirring, for 10 minutes or until soft. Add the garlic and both paprikas and cook, stirring, for 1 minute.

3 Add the saffron mixture, tomato and stock to the pan. Increase the heat to high. Bring to the boil, reduce the heat and cook gently for 20 minutes.

4 Stir in the chicken and chickpeas, season to taste with salt and freshly ground black pepper and cook for 3–4 minutes or until heated through. Serve immediately, sprinkled with the parsley, and accompanied by the toasted sourdough.

Thai prawn, pumpkin & coconut soup

Preparation time: 20 minutes
Cooking time: 30 minutes
Serves: 4

½ teaspoon shrimp paste
2 fresh long red chillies, chopped
¼ teaspoon white peppercorns
2 tablespoons sambal oelek (see tip)
2 garlic cloves
3 teaspoons vegetable oil
5 spring onions (scallions), sliced
125 ml (4 fl oz/½ cup) coconut cream
500 ml (17 fl oz/2 cups) good-quality
   chicken stock
875 ml (30 fl oz/3½ cups) coconut milk
750 g (1 lb 10 oz) pumpkin (winter
   squash), cut into 2 cm (¾ in) chunks
2 lemongrass stems, white part only,
   bruised
250 g (9 oz) raw small prawns (shrimp),
   peeled, deveined
1 tablespoon fish sauce
½ cup Thai basil leaves
coriander (cilantro) sprigs and chopped
   fresh red chilli, to serve

TIP: Sambal oelek is an
Indonesian red chilli paste
generally made with
chillies, sugar and salt.
You will find it in the
Asian or condiment section
of the supermarket.

1 Preheat grill (broiler) to high. Wrap the shrimp paste in a small piece of foil and place under preheated grill for 2 minutes or until aromatic, turning halfway through cooking.
2 Put the roasted shrimp paste in a small food processor with the chilli, peppercorns, sambal oelek, garlic and a pinch of salt, and process until smooth. Set aside.
3 Heat a wok over high heat, add the vegetable oil and swirl to coat the side. Cook the spring onion for 1–2 minutes or until lightly golden, then remove from the wok. Set aside.
4 Add the coconut cream to the wok and bring to the boil over high heat. Reduce the heat and simmer for 10 minutes or until the oil starts to separate from the cream—this is called cracking.
5 Stir the processed paste into the coconut cream and simmer over medium heat for 1–2 minutes or until aromatic. Add the stock, coconut milk, pumpkin, lemongrass and cooked spring onion, cover with a lid and simmer for 8–10 minutes or until the pumpkin is tender. Remove the lid, add the prawns and cook for another 2–3 minutes or until the prawns are just cooked through. Stir in the fish sauce and Thai basil and serve immediately, scattered with the coriander and chilli.

Lamb & spinach soup with paprika flat bread

Preparation time: 15 minutes
Cooking time: 30 minutes
Serves: 4

180 g (6¼ oz/¾ cup) risoni pasta
1 tablespoon olive oil
1 large brown onion, finely chopped
2 zucchini (courgettes), roughly chopped
1 celery stalk, thinly sliced
2 garlic cloves, crushed
1 x 10 cm (4 in) strip lemon zest, white pith removed
1 litre (35 fl oz/4 cups) good-quality chicken stock
250 ml (9 fl oz/1 cup) water
500 g (1 lb 2 oz) lamb fillets, trimmed, thinly sliced
50 g (1¾ oz) baby spinach leaves
2 tablespoons finely chopped mint leaves
lemon wedges, to serve

Paprika flat bread
2 rounds Lebanese bread
1 tablespoon olive oil
2 teaspoons sweet paprika

1 To make the paprika flat bread, preheat oven to 200°C (400°F/Gas 6). Place the bread on a baking tray in a single layer and brush with the combined olive oil and paprika. Bake for 5 minutes or until crisp and light golden. Transfer to a wire rack to cool. Break into large pieces.
2 Cook the pasta following the packet directions. Drain and set aside.
3 Meanwhile, heat the olive oil in a large saucepan over medium heat. Add the onion, zucchini and celery and cook, stirring, for 10 minutes or until the onion is soft. Add the garlic and cook for 1 minute.
4 Add the lemon zest, stock and water. Bring to the boil, then reduce the heat to low and simmer, uncovered, for 10 minutes. Stir in the lamb and spinach, then cook for 2 minutes or until the lamb is just cooked but still a little pink in the middle. Remove from the heat and stir in the mint and pasta. Discard the lemon zest. Serve immediately, with the paprika flat bread and lemon wedges.

Greek-style lamb meatball soup

Preparation time: 15 minutes
Cooking time: 20 minutes
Serves: 4

400 g (14 oz) minced (ground) lamb
40 g (1½ oz/⅓ cup) dry breadcrumbs
1 egg
40 g (1½ oz) feta cheese, finely crumbled
1 tablespoon finely chopped oregano
1½ tablespoons olive oil
1 brown onion, finely chopped
1 litre (35 fl oz/4 cups) good-quality vegetable stock
180 g (6¼ oz/¾ cup) risoni pasta
2 tablespoons freshly squeezed lemon juice
2 tablespoons finely chopped dill

1 Combine the mince, breadcrumbs, egg, feta and oregano in a large bowl. Season to taste with salt and freshly ground black pepper and mix well. Roll tablespoonfuls of the mixture into balls (you will make about 22 balls).

2 Heat 2 teaspoons of the olive oil in a large saucepan over medium heat. Add the onion and cook, stirring, for 3 minutes or until soft. Add the stock and bring to the boil over high heat. Add the pasta and simmer, covered, for 10 minutes.

3 Meanwhile, heat the remaining oil in a large non-stick frying pan over high heat. Cook the meatballs, turning, for 4–5 minutes or until browned. Drain on paper towel.

4 Add the meatballs to the soup mixture and simmer, covered, for another 3–4 minutes or until the pasta is al dente and the meatballs are cooked. Stir through the lemon juice and dill. Season to taste and serve immediately.

TIP: This soup is best served immediately as the risoni will continue to absorb the cooking liquid if left to stand, making the soup quite thick.

Pie-crust mushroom soup

Preparation time: 25 minutes (+ 10 minutes cooling time)
Cooking time: 50 minutes
Serves: 4

400 g (14 oz) large flat mushrooms
60 g (2¼ oz) butter
1 brown onion, finely chopped
1 garlic clove, crushed
30 g (1 oz) plain flour
750 ml (26 fl oz/3 cups) good-quality chicken stock
2 tablespoons thyme leaves
2 tablespoons sherry
250 ml (9 fl oz/1 cup) pouring (whipping) cream
2 sheets frozen puff pastry, thawed slightly
1 egg, lightly beaten

1 Preheat oven to 200°C (400°F/Gas 6). Roughly chop the mushrooms, including the stems.

2 Melt the butter in a large saucepan, add the onion and cook over medium heat for 8 minutes or until soft. Add the garlic and cook for 1 minute. Add the mushrooms and cook, stirring occasionally, for 10–15 minutes or until soft. Sprinkle with the flour and stir for 1 minute. Stir in the stock and thyme and bring to the boil. Reduce the heat and simmer, covered, for 10 minutes.

3 Cool slightly then transfer the soup in batches to a food processor and process until smooth.

4 Return the soup to the pan, stir in the sherry and cream then pour into four 250 ml (9 fl oz/1 cup) capacity ovenproof dishes (see tip). Set aside for 10 minutes or until the soup has cooled slightly.

5 Cut rounds of the pastry slightly larger than the dishes. Brush the edge of the dishes with a little water, cover each dish with a pastry round and press gently onto the edge to seal. Lightly brush the pastry with the beaten egg. Place the dishes on a baking tray and bake for 15 minutes or until golden and puffed. Serve immediately.

TIP: Small, deep dishes are better to use than wide, shallow ones in this recipe, as the pastry may sag into the soup.

Hearty pearl barley & borlotti bean soup

Preparation time: 15 minutes
Cooking time: 1 hour 10 minutes
Serves: 4

2 tablespoons vegetable oil
1 brown onion, cut into 2 cm (¾ in) thick slices
1 leek, pale section only, cut into 2 cm (¾ in) thick slices
1 carrot, thickly sliced
1 fresh bay leaf
1.25 litres (44 fl oz/5 cups) good-quality vegetable
   or chicken stock
400 g (14 oz) tin chopped tomatoes
2 tablespoons tomato paste (concentrated purée)
100 g (3½ oz/½ cup) pearl barley
¼ white cabbage (about 300 g/10½ oz), core removed,
   cut into 2 cm (¾ in) chunks
400 g (14 oz) tin borlotti (cranberry) beans, rinsed, drained
small basil leaves (optional), to serve

1 Heat the vegetable oil in a large saucepan over medium heat. Add the onion, leek and carrot and cook, stirring occasionally, for 8 minutes or until soft.
2 Stir in the bay leaf, stock, tomatoes, tomato paste, barley and cabbage. Bring to the boil, then reduce the heat to medium–low. Cover and simmer for 1 hour or until the barley is tender.
3 Season to taste with salt and freshly ground black pepper. Stir in the borlotti beans and bring back to a simmer.
4 Serve immediately, scattered with basil, if using.

Moroccan-style fish soup

Preparation time: 30 minutes
Cooking time: 30 minutes
Serves: 6

2 red capsicums (peppers)
1 fresh long red chilli
2 tablespoons extra virgin olive oil
1 brown onion, finely chopped
1 tablespoon tomato paste (concentrated purée)
2–3 teaspoons bought or home-made harissa
  (see page 18), to taste
4 garlic cloves, finely chopped
2 teaspoons ground cumin
625 ml (21½ fl oz/2½ cups) water
750 ml (26 fl oz/3 cups) good-quality fish stock
400 g (14 oz) tin chopped tomatoes
750 g (1 lb 10 oz) skinless, boneless firm white fish fillets,
  cut into 2 cm (¾ in) chunks
2 fresh bay leaves
2 tablespoons chopped coriander (cilantro) leaves
crusty bread (optional), to serve

1 Preheat grill (broiler) to high. Cut the capsicums into quarters and remove the membrane and seeds. Cut the chilli in half lengthways and remove the seeds. Cook the capsicum and chilli pieces, skin side up, under preheated grill until the skin blackens and blisters. Remove and place in a plastic bag, seal the bag and leave to steam until cool enough to handle. Peel the skin from the capsicum and the chilli and discard. Cut the flesh into thin strips. Set aside.

2 Heat the olive oil in a large saucepan over medium heat and cook the onion for 5 minutes or until soft. Add the tomato paste, harissa, garlic, cumin and 125 ml (4 fl oz/½ cup) of the water, then stir to combine. Add the stock, tomatoes and the remaining water. Bring to the boil, then reduce the heat and add the fish and bay leaves. Simmer gently for 5–7 minutes or until the fish is opaque and just cooked through.

3 Remove the fish with a slotted spoon and set aside. Discard the bay leaves. Cool slightly, add half the chopped coriander and transfer the soup in batches to a blender and process until smooth.

4 Return the soup to the pan, add the fish, capsicum and chilli and gently reheat. Season with salt and freshly ground black pepper. Serve immediately, sprinkled with the remaining coriander and accompanied by crusty bread, if using.

Goulash with herb dumplings

Preparation time: 30 minutes
Cooking time: 1 hour 30 minutes
Serves: 4–6

80 ml (2½ fl oz/⅓ cup) vegetable oil
2 brown onions, finely chopped
1 large carrot, peeled, finely chopped
2 celery stalks, finely chopped
2 garlic cloves, crushed
2 tablespoons tomato paste
  (concentrated pureé)
2 tablespoons sweet paprika
1½ teaspoons hot paprika
75 g (2¾ oz/½ cup) plain flour, seasoned,
  to dust
750 g (1 lb 10 oz) chuck steak, trimmed,
  cut into 1 cm (½ in) chunks
60 ml (2 fl oz/¼ cup) red wine vinegar

1.5 litres (52 fl oz/6 cups) good-quality
  salt-reduced beef stock
375 ml (13 fl oz/1½ cups) water
2 desiree or other all-purpose potatoes,
  peeled, cut into 1 cm (½ in) dice
2 fresh bay leaves

Herb dumplings
125 g (4½ oz) self-raising flour
50 g (1¾ oz) butter, chopped
1½ tablespoons chopped flat-leaf
  (Italian) parsley
1 tablespoon chopped oregano
½ teaspoon sea salt flakes
80 ml (2½ fl oz/⅓ cup) milk

1 Heat half the vegetable oil in a large saucepan over medium heat. Add the onion, carrot, celery and garlic and cook, stirring often, for 8 minutes or until soft. Add the tomato paste and both paprikas and cook, stirring often, for 2–3 minutes or until aromatic. Remove from the heat and set aside.

2 Put the flour in a large bowl, add the steak and toss to coat, shaking off any excess. Heat the remaining oil in a large frying pan over medium heat. Add the steak and cook, stirring often, for 4–5 minutes or until browned all over. Add to the onion mixture in the pan, reserving the frying pan.

3 Add the vinegar and 250 ml (9 fl oz/1 cup) of the stock to the frying pan and cook, scraping the base of the pan with a wooden spoon to loosen any stuck-on bits and bring the liquid to the boil. Add to the steak mixture in the saucepan with the remaining stock, the water, potato and bay leaves. Bring slowly to a simmer over medium heat. Reduce the heat to low and cook for 1 hour or until the steak is very tender.

4 Meanwhile, just before the soup is ready, to make the dumplings, place the flour in a bowl and use your fingertips to rub the butter in until the mixture resembles breadcrumbs. Add the herbs, sea salt and ½ teaspoon of freshly ground black pepper. Add the milk and use a flat-bladed knife to stir until a dough forms. Use floured hands to take slightly heaped teaspoonfuls of the dough and roll into balls.

5 Drop the dumplings into the simmering soup, cover the pan and cook for 10 minutes or until the dumplings are just cooked through. Taste and season if necessary. Serve immediately.

Spicy Vietnamese beef & pork noodle soup

Preparation time: 25 minutes (+ 30 minutes freezing time)
Cooking time: 25 minutes
Serves: 4

300 g (10½ oz) beef fillet steak
60 ml (2 fl oz/¼ cup) vegetable oil
300 g (10½ oz) pork leg steaks, cut into 2.5 cm (1 in) pieces
1 large brown onion, cut into thin wedges
2 litres (70 fl oz/8 cups) good-quality beef stock
500 ml (17 fl oz/2 cups) water
2 lemongrass stems
2 fresh long red chillies, sliced
2 tablespoons fish sauce
1 teaspoon ground dried shrimp
1 teaspoon sugar
400 g (14 oz) fresh thick rice noodles
230 g (8 oz/2 cups) bean sprouts, trimmed
1 cup firmly packed small mint leaves, to serve
⅔ cup small coriander (cilantro) leaves, to serve
thinly sliced fresh long red chilli (optional), to serve

1 Put the beef in the freezer for 20–30 minutes or until partially frozen, then cut into paper-thin slices across the grain. Cover and place in the fridge until needed.
2 Heat a wok until hot, add 1 tablespoon of the vegetable oil and swirl to coat the base and side. Stir-fry the pork in batches for 2–3 minutes or until browned. Remove from the wok and set aside.
3 Add another tablespoon of the oil to the wok and stir-fry the onion for 2–3 minutes or until starting to soften. Add the stock and water. Bruise one of the lemongrass stems and add it to the wok. Return the pork to the wok and bring to the boil, then reduce heat and simmer for 5 minutes or until the pork is just tender, occasionally skimming off any scum that rises to the surface.
4 Meanwhile, thinly slice the white part of the remaining lemongrass stem. Heat the remaining oil in a small frying pan over medium heat and cook the sliced lemongrass and chilli for 2–3 minutes or until aromatic. Set aside.
5 Remove the whole lemongrass stem from the broth. Stir in the sliced lemongrass and chilli, fish sauce, dried shrimp and sugar.
6 Put the rice noodles in a large heatproof bowl, cover with boiling water and gently separate the noodles. Drain immediately and rinse. Divide the noodles among warm serving bowls. Top with the beef slices and bean sprouts and ladle over the soup—the heat of the soup will cook the beef. Sprinkle with the mint, coriander and chilli, if using. Serve immediately.

Lamb & fusilli soup

Preparation time: 20 minutes
Cooking time: 45 minutes
Serves: 6–8

    2 tablespoons olive oil
    500 g (1 lb 2 oz) lean lamb leg, cut into 1.5 cm (⅝ in) chunks
    2 brown onions, finely chopped
    2 carrots, diced
    4 celery stalks, diced
    400 g (14 oz) tin chopped tomatoes
    2 litres (70 fl oz/8 cups) good-quality beef stock
    500 g (1 lb 2 oz) fusilli pasta
    chopped flat-leaf (Italian) parsley, to serve

1 Heat the olive oil in a large saucepan over medium–high heat and cook the lamb in two separate batches until well browned. Drain on paper towel. Set aside.

2 Reduce the heat to medium, add the onion to the pan and cook for 8 minutes or until soft. Return the meat to the pan with the carrot, celery, tomatoes and stock. Stir to combine and bring to the boil. Reduce the heat to low and simmer, covered, for 15 minutes.

3 Add the pasta and stir to prevent the pasta from sticking to the pan. Simmer, uncovered, for another 10 minutes or until the lamb and pasta are tender. Serve immediately, sprinkled with the parsley.

Spanish-style rice, mussel, prawn & chorizo soup

Preparation time: 45 minutes
Cooking time: 50 minutes
Serves: 4

1 kg (2 lb 4 oz) black mussels, scrubbed,
  debearded (see tip)
250 ml (9 fl oz/1 cup) dry sherry
1 tablespoon olive oil
1 red onion, chopped
200 g (7 oz) chorizo, thinly sliced
4 garlic cloves, crushed
100 g (3½ oz/½ cup) long-grain
  white rice
400 g (14 oz) tin chopped tomatoes
2 litres (70 fl oz/8 cups) good-quality
  chicken stock
½ teaspoon saffron threads
2 fresh bay leaves
1 tablespoon chopped oregano
500 g (1 lb 2 oz) raw prawns (shrimp),
  peeled, deveined, tails left intact
¼ cup chopped flat-leaf (Italian) parsley

TIP: Prepare the mussels by scrubbing the shells and pulling out the hairy beards. Discard any that have broken shells, or ones that don't close when tapped on the bench. Rinse well.

1 Put the mussels in a saucepan with the sherry and cook, covered, over high heat for 4–5 minutes or until the mussels have opened. Strain the liquid into a bowl. (Discard any unopened mussels.) Remove all but eight mussels from their shells and discard the empty shells.
2 Heat the olive oil in a large saucepan over medium heat, add the onion and cook for 5–8 minutes or until softened but not browned. Add the chorizo and cook for 3–5 minutes or until browned, then add the garlic and cook for another minute. Add the rice and stir to coat with the onion mixture. Add the reserved cooking liquid and cook for 1 minute, then add the tomatoes, stock, saffron, bay leaves and oregano. Bring to the boil then reduce the heat and simmer, covered, for 25 minutes.
3 Add the prawns to the soup, cover with a lid and cook for 3 minutes or until just tender. Stir in all the mussels and parsley and heat through. Ladle the soup into serving bowls and serve immediately.

Spinach, lentil & lemon soup

Preparation time: 20 minutes
Cooking time: 35 minutes
Serves: 4

1 tablespoon olive oil
1 large brown onion, finely chopped
2 celery stalks, finely chopped
200 g (7 oz) pancetta, cut into thick strips
2 garlic cloves, crushed
3 lemon thyme sprigs
500 g (1 lb 2 oz) potatoes, peeled, chopped
800 g (1 lb 12 oz) tinned brown lentils, rinsed, drained
1 litre (35 fl oz/4 cups) good-quality chicken stock
500 ml (17 fl oz/2 cups) water
1 bunch (about 310 g/11 oz) English spinach (see tip)
80 ml (2½ fl oz/⅓ cup) freshly squeezed lemon juice

Chilli oil
1 fresh long red chilli, finely chopped
1½ tablespoons flat-leaf (Italian) parsley,
    finely chopped
2 tablespoons extra virgin olive oil

TIP: You will need about 110 g (3¾ oz) trimmed, shredded spinach for this recipe.

1 To make the chilli oil, combine all the ingredients in a small bowl. Set aside.

2 Heat the olive oil in a large saucepan over medium heat. Add the onion, celery and pancetta and cook, stirring, for 10 minutes or until the vegetables are soft. Add the garlic and thyme and cook for 1 minute or until aromatic.

3 Add the potato, lentils, stock and water. Bring to the boil, then reduce the heat to low and simmer, uncovered, for 20 minutes or until the potato is very tender. Meanwhile, trim and shred the English spinach. Remove the soup from the heat and stir in the spinach and lemon juice. Serve immediately, drizzled with the chilli oil.

On the lighter side

Spring minestrone

Preparation time: 20 minutes
Cooking time: 20 minutes
Serves: 4

1 tablespoon olive oil
1 garlic clove, thinly sliced
6 spring onions (scallions), sliced
1 carrot, cut into 1 cm (½ in) dice
1.2 litres (42 fl oz) good-quality chicken stock
100 g (3½ oz) green beans, cut into 1.5 cm (⅝ in) lengths
1 zucchini (courgette), cut into 1 cm (½ in) dice
65 g (2½ oz/½ cup) macaroni (pasta elbows)
3 ripe tomatoes, peeled, seeded, flesh cut into 1 cm (½ in) dice
180 g (6¼ oz) asparagus, trimmed, cut into 2 cm (¾ in) lengths
400 g (14 oz) tin cannellini beans, rinsed, drained
75 g (2¾ oz/½ cup) fresh or frozen peas
160 g (5¾ oz/⅔ cup) rocket pesto (see page 118), to serve
grated parmesan cheese (optional), to serve

1 Place a saucepan over medium–low heat. Add the olive oil, garlic, spring onion and carrot and cook, stirring frequently, for 5–7 minutes just to soften but not colour.
2 Add the stock, increase the heat to high and bring to the boil. Add the green beans, zucchini and pasta and boil gently for 4 minutes.
3 Add the tomato, asparagus, cannellini beans and peas and cook for another 6 minutes or until the pasta is al dente. Serve immediately, topped with the pesto and the parmesan, if using.

Green pea soup

Preparation time: 20 minutes (+ 2 hours soaking time)
Cooking time: 1 hour 40 minutes
Serves: 4–6

330 g (11½ oz/1½ cups) dried green split peas
2 tablespoons olive oil
1 brown onion, finely chopped
1 celery stalk, thinly sliced
1 carrot, thinly sliced
1 tablespoon ground cumin
1 tablespoon ground coriander
2 teaspoons finely grated fresh ginger
1.25 litres (44 fl oz/5 cups) good-quality vegetable stock
280 g (10 oz/2 cups) frozen peas
1 tablespoon chopped mint
plain yoghurt or light sour cream, to serve

1 Soak the split peas in cold water for 2 hours. Drain the peas well.
2 Heat the olive oil in a large saucepan, add the onion, celery and carrot and cook over medium heat for 3 minutes, stirring occasionally, until soft but not browned. Stir in the cumin, coriander and ginger and cook for 1 minute. Add the soaked split peas and stock. Bring to the boil, then reduce the heat to low. Simmer, covered, for 1½ hours, stirring occasionally.
3 Stir the frozen peas into the soup. Cool the soup slightly then transfer in batches to a food processor and process until smooth. Return the soup to the saucepan and reheat over medium heat. Season to taste with salt and freshly ground black pepper, then stir in the mint. Serve topped with a swirl of yoghurt or sour cream.

Chinese lamb soup with rice noodles

Preparation time: 20 minutes (+ 30 minutes standing time)
Cooking time: 25 minutes
Serves: 4

15 dried shiitake mushrooms
500 g (1 lb 2 oz) lamb leg steaks, trimmed,
  cut into 1 cm (½ in) pieces
2½ tablespoons Chinese rice wine or dry sherry
1 tablespoon dark soy sauce
2 garlic cloves, crushed
2½ teaspoons very finely chopped fresh ginger
½ teaspoon sesame oil
1.5 litres (52 fl oz/6 cups) good-quality chicken stock
2½ tablespoons grated palm sugar (jaggery)
60 ml (2 fl oz/¼ cup) hoisin sauce
1 cinnamon stick
2 star anise
2 x 1 cm (½ in) wide strips orange zest, white pith removed
100 g (3½ oz) dried rice vermicelli
2 spring onions (scallions), trimmed, thinly diagonally sliced, to serve
½ cup coriander (cilantro) leaves, roughly chopped, to serve

1 Put the mushrooms in a small bowl and pour enough boiling water over to just cover. Stand for 30 minutes or until soft. Drain well, reserving the liquid, and slice the mushrooms.
2 Meanwhile, combine the lamb, half the rice wine, half the soy sauce and the garlic, ginger and sesame oil in a bowl and toss to combine well. Cover and stand at room temperature for 30 minutes.
3 Combine the remaining wine and soy sauce in a large saucepan with the mushroom liquid, stock, sugar, hoisin sauce, cinnamon stick, star anise and orange zest and slowly bring to a simmer. Cover and cook over low heat for 15 minutes to allow the flavours to develop. Remove the spices and the orange zest and discard.
4 Cook the noodles in a saucepan of boiling water for 2 minutes or until tender. Drain well.
5 Add the undrained lamb and the mushrooms to the broth in the pan and poach gently for 2–3 minutes or until the lamb is only just cooked through—do not allow the broth to boil or the lamb will be tough. Stir in the noodles and cook for 1 minute to heat through.
6 To serve, divide the soup among warmed serving bowls. Serve immediately, topped with the spring onion and coriander.

Rustic lamb, vegetable & mint soup

Preparation time: 20 minutes
Cooking time: 25 minutes
Serves: 4

1 tablespoon olive oil
6 lamb loin chops (about 1 kg/2 lb 4 oz in total),
   deboned, trimmed, cut into 2 cm (¾ in) pieces
   (see tip)
60 ml (2 fl oz/¼ cup) white wine
500 g (1 lb 2 oz) potatoes, peeled, cut into
   1 cm (½ in) pieces
2 carrots, peeled, sliced
1 red onion, cut into wedges
2 mint sprigs
250 ml (9 fl oz/1 cup) good-quality
   vegetable stock
500 ml (17 fl oz/2 cups) water
200 g (7 oz) Italian flat beans (see tip), trimmed,
   cut into 3 cm (1¼ in) lengths
1 cup lightly packed mint leaves, finely chopped

TIPS: You will need about 400 g (14 oz) boneless lamb meat for this recipe.

Italian flat beans are available from selected greengrocers. If unavailable, you can use green beans instead.

1 Heat the olive oil in a large saucepan over high heat. Cook the lamb, turning occasionally, for 3 minutes or until browned. Remove the lamb and set aside. Discard the cooking oil.
2 Add the wine to the saucepan and scrape the base with a wooden spoon to loosen any stuck-on bits. Cook for 1 minute or until the wine is slightly reduced.
3 Add the potato, carrot, onion, mint sprigs, stock and water. Bring to the boil over high heat. Reduce the heat and simmer, covered, for 10 minutes. Add the beans and simmer, covered, for 5 minutes or until the vegetables are tender.
4 Discard the mint sprigs, then stir through the chopped mint and the lamb. Season to taste with salt and freshly ground black pepper and serve immediately.

Quick vegetable & cannellini bean soup

Preparation time: 10 minutes
Cooking time: 20 minutes
Serves: 4

1 tablespoon olive oil
1 brown onion, finely chopped
2 carrots, chopped
250 g (9 oz) leg ham, diced
400 g (14 oz) tin cannellini beans, rinsed, drained
1.25 litres (44 fl oz/5 cups) water
80 g (2¾ oz/½ cup) macaroni (pasta elbows)
2 zucchini (courgettes), chopped
⅓ cup shredded basil leaves, to serve
shaved parmesan cheese, to serve

1 Heat the olive oil in a large saucepan over medium heat. Add the onion and carrot and cook for 8 minutes or until soft.
2 Add the ham, beans and water and bring to the boil over high heat. Add the pasta and simmer for 5 minutes. Add the zucchini and simmer for another 5 minutes or until the pasta is al dente. Serve sprinkled with the basil and parmesan.

TIP: Vary the vegetables according to the season. You could use fennel, celery, turnip or sweet potato in place of or in addition to the zucchini.

Simple mushroom soup

Preparation time: 10 minutes
Cooking time: 25 minutes
Serves: 4

60 g (2¼ oz) butter
2 onions, chopped
500 g (1 lb 2 oz) button mushrooms, chopped
35 g (1¼ oz/¼ cup) plain flour
500 ml (17 fl oz/2 cups) milk
375 ml (13 fl oz/1½ cups) good-quality vegetable stock
sour cream, to serve
chopped flat-leaf (Italian) parsley, to serve

1 Heat the butter in a medium saucepan and cook the onion over medium heat for 5 minutes or until lightly golden. Add the mushrooms and cook, stirring often, for another 5 minutes.
2 Add the flour and stir for 1 minute. Stir in the milk and stock. Reduce the heat and simmer, uncovered, for 10–15 minutes or until the soup has thickened and the mushrooms are tender.
3 Serve topped with a dollop of sour cream sprinkled with the parsley.

Asian beef & noodle soup

Preparation time: 10 minutes (+ 30 minutes standing time)
Cooking time: 30 minutes
Serves: 4

2 dried shiitake mushrooms
250 ml (9 fl oz/1 cup) boiling water
1 tablespoon peanut oil
1 spring onion (scallion), trimmed, thinly sliced
3 cm (1¼ in) piece fresh ginger, peeled, thinly sliced
2 tablespoons Chinese rice wine
2 tablespoons soy sauce
1 star anise
1 litre (35 fl oz/4 cups) good-quality salt-reduced beef stock
600 g (1 lb 5 oz) rump steak
600 g (1 lb 5 oz) fresh rice noodles
1 bunch (350 g/12 oz) baby bok choy (pak choy), thickly sliced
50 g (1¾ oz) snow peas (mangetout), thinly sliced
1 tablespoon crisp fried Asian shallots
sesame oil and chilli sauce, to serve

1 Put the mushrooms in a small bowl and pour over the boiling water. Stand for 30 minutes or until the mushrooms are soft. Drain well, reserving the liquid. Remove the stems and slice thinly.

2 Heat 2 teaspoons of the peanut oil in a heavy-based saucepan over medium heat. Add the spring onion, ginger and mushrooms and cook, stirring, for 30 seconds. Increase the heat to high, add the rice wine, soy sauce, star anise, stock and the reserved mushroom liquid and bring to the boil. Simmer for 2–3 minutes, then reduce the heat to low and simmer, uncovered, for 15 minutes.

3 Strain the stock, reserving the liquid. Discard the solids. Return the liquid to the saucepan and simmer to keep warm.

4 Put the remaining oil in a medium heavy-based frying pan over high heat. When the oil is hot, add the steak and cook for 2–3 minutes on each side. Remove the steak from the pan and set aside for 5 minutes, then slice thinly.

5 Add the bok choy to a saucepan of boiling water and cook for 10–20 seconds or until tender, crisp and bright green. Drain and refresh under cold running water.

6 Put the noodles in a heatproof bowl. Pour over boiling water and use tongs to gently separate the noodles. Drain immediately.

7 Divide the bok choy, snow peas, noodles and beef among serving bowls. Ladle the soup over and garnish with the Asian shallots. Serve immediately with the sesame oil and chilli sauce passed separately.

Thai lemongrass broth with mussels

Preparation time: 20 minutes
Cooking time: 25 minutes
Serves: 4

1 tablespoon vegetable oil
5 spring onions (scallions), thinly sliced
2 garlic cloves, crushed
750 ml (26 fl oz/3 cups) good-quality chicken or fish stock
750 ml (26 fl oz/3 cups) water
2½ tablespoons sliced fresh galangal or ginger
4 lemongrass stems, white part only, bruised
2 fresh long red chillies, halved lengthways
6 kaffir lime leaves, crushed
1.5 kg (3 lb 5 oz) black mussels, scrubbed, debearded (see tip)
2 tablespoons roughly chopped coriander (cilantro) leaves
lime wedges, shredded kaffir lime leaves and
    sliced fresh red chilli (optional), to serve

1 Heat a wok over medium heat, add the vegetable oil and swirl to coat the base and side of the wok. Cook the spring onion and garlic for 1 minute or until soft. Add the stock, water, galangal, lemongrass, chilli and lime leaves. Bring to the boil, reduce the heat and simmer for 15 minutes.

2 Add the mussels, cover with a lid and bring to the boil over high heat. Reduce the heat to medium and cook for 4–5 minutes, tossing occasionally, or until the mussels have opened. (Discard any unopened mussels.)

3 Stir in half the coriander. Serve the broth and mussels immediately, sprinkled with the remaining coriander. Serve with the lime wedges, lime leaves and chilli passed separately, if using.

TIP: Prepare the mussels by scrubbing the shells and pulling out the hairy beards. Discard any that have broken shells, or ones that don't close when tapped on the bench. Rinse well.

Chicken, asparagus & egg noodle soup

Preparation time: 15 minutes
Cooking time: 15 minutes
Serves: 4

> 200 g (7 oz) fresh thin egg noodles
> 200 g (7 oz) asparagus, trimmed
> 4 spring onions (scallions)
> 1.5 litres (52 fl oz/6 cups) good-quality
>   salt-reduced chicken stock
> 500 ml (17 fl oz/2 cups) water
> 6 thin slices fresh ginger
> 1 tablespoon light soy sauce, or to taste
> 600 g (1 lb 5 oz) skinless chicken breast fillets,
>   trimmed, thinly sliced
> 150 g (5½ oz) baby spinach leaves
> lemon cheeks or wedges, to serve

1 Put the noodles in a colander and place the colander in a heatproof bowl. Pour over some boiling water. Use a fork to briefly loosen the noodles and then drain immediately. Set aside.

2 Remove the top third of the asparagus and cut in half lengthways. Cut the remaining stalks into 1 cm (½ in) rounds. Set aside.

3 Remove the green tops of the spring onions and thinly slice diagonally. Set aside. Thinly slice the remaining white part of the spring onion into rounds.

4 Place the stock, water, ginger and the white part of the spring onion in a large saucepan over high heat and bring to the boil. Reduce the heat to medium and simmer for 5 minutes. Add the soy sauce.

5 Add the chicken and asparagus and simmer for 2 minutes. Stir through the spinach leaves and the noodles and simmer for 2 minutes or until the chicken is just cooked.

6 Use tongs to divide the noodles and chicken evenly among serving bowls then ladle over the broth. Serve immediately, topped with the spring onion greens and the lemon passed separately.

Japanese udon miso soup with chicken

Preparation time: 15 minutes (+ 30 minutes soaking time)
Cooking time: 10 minutes
Serves: 4–6

8 dried shiitake mushrooms
250 ml (9 fl oz/1 cup) boiling water
400 g (14 oz) fresh udon noodles
1 litre (35 fl oz/4 cups) good-quality chicken stock
1 litre (35 fl oz/4 cups) water
600 g (1 lb 5 oz) skinless chicken breast fillets,
  cut into 1.5 cm (⅝ in) thick strips
300 g (10½ oz) baby bok choy (pak choy), halved lengthways
60 g (2¼ oz/¼ cup) white miso paste
2 teaspoons dashi granules (see tip)
1 tablespoon wakame flakes or other seaweed
150 g (5½ oz) silken firm tofu, cut into 1 cm (½ in) dice
3 spring onions (scallions), sliced diagonally, to serve

1 Soak the mushrooms in the boiling water for
30 minutes. Squeeze dry, reserving the soaking liquid.
Discard the woody stalks and thinly slice the caps.
Set aside.

2 Bring a large saucepan of water to the boil and cook
the noodles for 1–2 minutes or until just tender. Drain
immediately and rinse under cold water. Set aside.

3 Put the stock and water into a wok and bring to the
boil over high heat. Reduce the heat, add the chicken
and simmer gently for 2–3 minutes or until almost
cooked through.

4 Add the mushrooms and cook for 1 minute. Add the
bok choy halves and simmer for another 1 minute or until
beginning to wilt.

5 Remove from the heat, add the miso paste, dashi
granules, wakame and reserved mushroom liquid and
stir to dissolve the dashi and miso paste. Gently stir in
the tofu. Divide the noodles among serving bowls then
ladle the hot soup over. Serve the soup scattered with
the spring onion.

TIP: Dashi granules are
used to make Japanese
soup stock. They are
available from the
Asian section of selected
supermarkets or from
Asian grocery stores.

Fast & simple

Mexican cream of corn soup

Preparation time: 10 minutes
Cooking time: 30 minutes
Serves: 4

2 tablespoons vegetable oil
1 large brown onion, chopped
2½ teaspoons ground cumin
2 teaspoons dried oregano
1 teaspoon chilli powder (optional)
900 g (2 lb/6 cups) frozen corn kernels
1 litre (35 fl oz/4 cups) good-quality salt-reduced chicken stock
300 g (10½ oz) sour cream
125 g (4½ oz/½ cup) mild Mexican salsa, or to taste
coriander (cilantro) sprigs, to serve
100 g (3½ oz) corn chips, to serve

1 Heat the vegetable oil in a large saucepan over medium heat. Add the onion and cook, stirring, for 5 minutes or until soft. Add the cumin, oregano and chilli, if using. Cook, stirring, for another minute, or until aromatic.

2 Add the corn and reduce the heat to medium–low. Cover the pan and cook for 10 minutes, stirring occasionally, or until the corn is just tender.

3 Add the stock, bring to a simmer then cook over low heat for 10 minutes or until the corn is very tender. Season to taste with salt and freshly ground black pepper.

4 Cool slightly then transfer the soup in batches to a food processor or blender and process until roughly puréed. Return to the saucepan, whisk in half the sour cream and reheat without simmering. Serve immediately, topped with the remaining sour cream, the salsa and coriander. Pass the corn chips separately for adding to the soup as desired.

Cannellini bean & silverbeet soup

Preparation time: 10 minutes
Cooking time: 15 minutes
Serves: 4

2 tablespoons olive oil
3 garlic cloves, thinly sliced
4 anchovy fillets, finely chopped
1 litre (35 fl oz/4 cups) good-quality chicken stock
2 x 400 g (14 oz) tins cannellini beans, rinsed, drained
400 g (14 oz) tin chopped tomatoes
1 bunch (1 kg/2 lb 4 oz) silverbeet (Swiss chard) (see tip),
   leaves trimmed, washed, finely shredded (see tip)

1 Heat the olive oil in a large saucepan over medium heat. Add the garlic and anchovies and cook, stirring, for 3–4 minutes or until the garlic is golden.
2 Stir in the stock, beans and tomatoes and simmer, covered, for 10 minutes.
3 Stir in the silverbeet and simmer for 1 minute or until wilted. Season with salt and freshly ground black pepper and serve.

TIPS: You will need about 340 g (12 oz) shredded silverbeet for this recipe.

Keep the white silverbeet stalks for a quick pasta sauce with garlic, tinned tomatoes, bacon and chilli.

Crab bisque

Preparation time: 10 minutes
Cooking time: 15 minutes
Serves: 6

50 g (1¾ oz) butter
1 brown onion, finely chopped
400 g (14 oz) cooked crabmeat (see tip)
500 ml (17 fl oz/2 cups) milk
500 ml (17 fl oz/2 cups) pouring (whipping) cream
1 tablespoon whisky
freshly ground white pepper
2 tablespoons finely snipped chives

TIP: Cooked crabmeat is available from good seafood suppliers or selected supermarkets in the seafood department.

1 Melt the butter in a large saucepan over medium heat. Add the onion and cook, stirring, for 5 minutes or until soft.

2 Add the crab and cook, stirring, for 1 minute.

3 Add the milk and cream and bring to a simmer. Simmer gently for 5 minutes.

4 Stir in the whisky and season with salt and white pepper. Serve immediately, sprinkled with the chives.

Broccoli soup

Preparation time: 10 minutes
Cooking time: 35 minutes
Serves: 4

30 g (1 oz) butter
1 leek, pale section only, thinly sliced
200 g (7 oz) speck (see tip), chopped
2 garlic cloves, crushed
4 thyme sprigs
400 g (14 oz) all-purpose potatoes, peeled,
  cut into 1 cm (½ in) pieces
1 litre (35 fl oz/4 cups) good-quality salt-reduced
  chicken stock
500 ml (17 fl oz/2 cups) water
650 g (1 lb 7 oz) broccoli florets (see tip), finely chopped
60 ml (2 fl oz/¼ cup) pouring (whipping) cream, to serve
crisp sage leaves (see page 117), to serve

TIPS: Speck is a European-style bacon available in selected supermarkets and from butchers.

You will need 3 medium heads (900 g/2 lb) of broccoli for this recipe.

1 Melt the butter in a large saucepan over medium heat. Add the leek and speck and cook, stirring, for 10 minutes or until soft. Add the garlic and thyme and cook, stirring, for 1 minute. Add the potato and cook, stirring, for 5 minutes.

2 Add the stock, water and broccoli. Bring to the boil, then reduce the heat to low and simmer, uncovered, for 10–15 minutes or until the potato is very soft. Remove the thyme sprigs.

3 Cool slightly then transfer the soup in batches to a food processor and process until smooth. Return the soup to the saucepan and reheat over medium heat. Season to taste with salt and freshly ground black pepper. Serve the soup drizzled with the cream and topped with the crisp sage leaves.

Capsicum & tomato soup with couscous

Preparation time: 10 minutes
Cooking time: 20 minutes
Serves: 4

2 x 270 g (9½ oz) jars chargrilled red capsicums (peppers) in oil
1 tablespoon olive oil
1 red onion, chopped
2 garlic cloves, chopped
60 g (2¼ oz/¼ cup) tomato paste (concentrated purée)
2 x 400 g (14 oz) tins chopped tomatoes
1 litre (35 fl oz/4 cups) good-quality chicken stock
130 g (4½ oz/⅔ cup) couscous
plain yoghurt, to serve
chopped coriander (cilantro) leaves, to serve

1 Drain the oil from the capsicum (you will need about 400 g/14 oz capsicum). Put the capsicum in a food processor and pulse until almost smooth.

2 Put the olive oil and onion in a large saucepan over medium heat and cook, stirring occasionally, for 5 minutes or until soft. Add the garlic and cook for 1 minute or until aromatic. Add the tomato paste and cook, stirring, for another 2 minutes.

3 Add the tomatoes, stock and puréed capsicum to the pan, increase the heat to high and bring to the boil. Reduce heat and simmer for 5 minutes.

4 Stir through the couscous and simmer for 2 minutes. Turn off the heat and set aside for 3 minutes or until the couscous is tender. Season with salt. Serve immediately, topped with the yoghurt and coriander.

Fast pork & prawn laksa

Preparation time: 20 minutes
Cooking time: 15 minutes
Serves: 4

200 g (7 oz) dried rice stick noodles
2½ tablespoons vegetable oil
230 g (8 oz) jar laksa paste
375 ml (13 fl oz/1½ cups) water
1 lemongrass stem, bruised, tied in a knot
350 g (12 oz) pork fillet, trimmed, thinly sliced
300 g (10½ oz) peeled, deveined raw prawns (shrimp)
2 x 270 ml (9½ fl oz) tins coconut cream
200 g (7 oz) fried tofu puffs, sliced, to serve
115 g (4 oz/1 cup) bean sprouts, trimmed, to serve
sliced fresh long red chilli, to serve
coriander (cilantro) sprigs, to serve
crisp fried shallots, to serve

1 Cook the noodles in boiling water for 6 minutes following the packet directions until just tender. Drain well, drizzle with 2 teaspoons of the vegetable oil, toss to coat the noodles and set aside.

2 Meanwhile, heat the remaining oil in a large saucepan over medium heat. Add the laksa paste and cook, stirring, for 2–3 minutes or until aromatic. Add the water and lemongrass and bring to the boil.

3 Reduce the heat to medium–low. Add the pork and prawns to the pan and cook for about 3 minutes or until just tender. Add the coconut cream and cook, stirring, for 2–3 minutes or until heated through. Serve immediately, topped with the tofu, bean sprouts, chilli, coriander and crisp fried shallots.

Fast red lentil & capsicum soup

Preparation time: 10 minutes
Cooking time: 20 minutes
Serves: 4

2 brown onions
305 g (10¾ oz/1½ cups) split red lentils, rinsed, drained
500 ml (17 fl oz/2 cups) good-quality chicken stock
500 ml (17 fl oz/2 cups) water
2 tablespoons olive oil
1 large red capsicum (pepper), seeded, thinly sliced
4 garlic cloves, thinly sliced

1 Roughly chop one onion and thinly slice the other onion.

2 Combine the lentils, chopped onion, stock and water in a large saucepan over high heat. Bring to the boil, then reduce the heat to medium. Simmer for 10 minutes or until tender. Skim the foam from the surface and discard.

3 Cool slightly then transfer the soup in batches to a food processor or blender and process until smooth. Return the soup to the saucepan and reheat over medium heat.

4 Meanwhile, heat the olive oil in a large frying pan over medium heat. Cook the capsicum, stirring, for 5 minutes. Add the sliced onion and the garlic and cook, stirring, for 10 minutes or until soft and the onion starts to caramelise.

5 Stir half the onion mixture through the soup. Season to taste with salt and freshly ground black pepper. Serve the soup topped with the remaining onion mixture.

Asparagus soup

Preparation time: 10 minutes
Cooking time: 20 minutes
Serves: 4

30 g (1 oz) butter
1 large brown onion, chopped
2 garlic cloves, crushed
4 thyme sprigs
1 litre (35 fl oz/4 cups) good-quality
   salt-reduced chicken stock
700 g (1 lb 9 oz/4 bunches) asparagus,
   trimmed, chopped (see tip)
125 ml (4 fl oz/½ cup) reduced-fat
   thickened (whipping) cream
freshly ground white pepper
gremolata (see page 117), to serve

TIP: You will need about 450 g (1 lb) trimmed asparagus for this recipe.

1 Melt the butter in a large saucepan over medium heat. Add the onion and cook, stirring, for 5 minutes or until soft. Add the garlic and thyme and cook, stirring, for 1 minute.

2 Add the stock and asparagus. Bring to the boil, reduce the heat to low and simmer, uncovered, for 10 minutes or until the asparagus is very soft. Remove the thyme sprigs.

3 Cool slightly then transfer the soup in batches to a food processor and process until smooth. Return the soup to the saucepan over medium–low heat and add the cream. Cook, stirring, for 3 minutes or until heated through (do not boil). Season to taste with salt and white pepper. Serve sprinkled with the gremolata.

Curried zucchini soup

Preparation time: 20 minutes
Cooking time: 20 minutes
Serves: 4

50 g (1¾ oz) butter
1 kg (2 lb 4 oz) zucchini (courgettes), chopped
1 brown onion, chopped
2 teaspoons mild curry powder
500 ml (17 fl oz/2 cups) good-quality chicken stock
500 ml (17 fl oz/2 cups) water
plain yoghurt, to serve
naan bread, toasted, to serve

1 Melt the butter in a large saucepan over medium heat. Stir in the zucchini and onion and cook, covered, for 10 minutes, stirring occasionally, or until soft.

2 Stir in the curry powder. Add the stock and water. Bring to the boil over high heat. Reduce the heat and simmer, covered, for 5 minutes or until almost tender.

3 Stand for 10 minutes to cool slightly and for the zucchini to finish cooking. Transfer the soup in batches to a food processor or blender and process until smooth. Return the soup to the saucepan and reheat over medium heat. Season to taste with salt and freshly ground black pepper. Serve with the yoghurt and naan bread.

Lemon-scented broth with tortellini

Preparation time: 10 minutes
Cooking time: 20 minutes
Serves: 4

1 lemon
125 ml (4 fl oz/½ cup) white wine
440 g (15½ oz) tin chicken consommé
750 ml (26 fl oz/3 cups) water
375 g (13 oz) fresh veal or chicken tortellini
⅓ cup chopped flat-leaf (Italian) parsley, to serve
finely grated parmesan cheese, to serve

1 Use a vegetable peeler to peel wide strips of zest from the lemon. Remove the white pith using a small, sharp knife. Cut three of the wide pieces into fine strips and set aside for a garnish.
2 Combine the remaining wide strips of lemon zest, wine, consommé and water in a large saucepan. Cook for 10 minutes over low heat.
3 Remove the lemon zest pieces and bring to the boil. Add the tortellini and season with freshly ground black pepper. Cook for 6–7 minutes or until the pasta is al dente. Divide the tortellini among shallow serving bowls and ladle over the broth. Serve sprinkled with the parsley, reserved lemon zest strips and parmesan.

Carrot soup

Preparation time: 10 minutes
Cooking time: 30 minutes
Serves: 4

60 ml (2 fl oz/¼ cup) olive oil
1 brown onion, chopped
1 kg (2 lb 4 oz) carrots, cut into 1 cm (½ in) pieces
1 tablespoon roughly chopped fresh ginger
2 star anise
1.125 litres (39 fl oz/4½ cups) good-quality chicken stock
250 ml (9 fl oz/1 cup) pouring (whipping) cream
sour cream, to serve
chopped flat-leaf (Italian) parsley, to serve
grilled Turkish bread, cut lengthways into fingers, to serve

1 Put the olive oil, onion, carrot, ginger and star anise in a large saucepan over medium heat and cook, stirring frequently, for 10 minutes or until the onion is soft but not coloured.

2 Add the stock, increase the heat to high and bring to the boil. Reduce the heat and simmer for 15 minutes or until the carrot is very tender.

3 Remove the star anise and discard. Cool slightly then transfer the soup in batches to a food processor or blender and process until smooth. Return the soup to the saucepan over medium heat, add the cream and stir to combine. Bring just to a simmer. Season with salt and freshly ground black pepper. Serve topped with the sour cream and parsley and accompanied by the grilled bread.

Cold avocado soup with lime-pickled onions

Preparation time: 25 minutes
Cooking time: 10 minutes
Serves: 4

1½ tablespoons avocado or other vegetable oil
1 brown onion, chopped
1½ teaspoons ground cumin
1½ teaspoons ground coriander
1 garlic clove, crushed
500 g (1 lb 2 oz) ripe Hass avocados (about 3 small),
  peeled, stones removed, chopped
1 litre (35 fl oz/4 cups) good-quality chicken or vegetable stock, chilled
60 ml (2 fl oz/¼ cup) freshly squeezed lime juice, or to taste

Lime-pickled onions
1 small red onion, halved, very thinly sliced
2 tablespoons freshly squeezed lime juice
2 teaspoons caster sugar
1 teaspoon sea salt flakes

1 To make the lime-pickled onions, put all the ingredients in a small bowl and toss to combine well. Cover and stand at room temperature for 30 minutes to allow the onions to 'pickle'.
2 Meanwhile, heat the oil in a small saucepan, add the onion, cover and cook, stirring occasionally, for 6 minutes or until soft. Add the spices and cook, stirring, for 1 minute or until aromatic. Remove from the heat and cool.
3 Put the onion mixture, garlic, avocado, stock and lime juice in a food processor or blender and process until a smooth purée forms. Season to taste with salt and freshly ground black pepper, and a little extra lime juice, if necessary. Serve immediately, topped with the lime-pickled onions.

Italian chicken dumpling soup

Preparation time: 20 minutes
Cooking time: 10 minutes
Serves: 4

350 g (12 oz) minced (ground) chicken
75 g (2¾ oz/1 cup, firmly packed) fresh breadcrumbs
70 g (2½ oz/⅔ cup) finely grated parmesan cheese
1½ tablespoons rinsed, chopped capers
2 tablespoons chopped basil
1 egg yolk
1.25 litres (44 fl oz/5 cups) good-quality
   chicken consommé or home-made chicken stock
chopped flat-leaf (Italian) parsley, to serve

1 To make the dumplings, use your hands to mix all the ingredients except the egg yolk, consommé and parsley in a medium bowl and combine well. Season with salt and freshly ground black pepper, then add the egg yolk and mix to combine.

2 Take heaped teaspoonfuls of the mixture and use your hands to roll into balls, placing the dumplings in a single layer on a plate or tray as you roll. Cover and refrigerate until required.

3 Bring the consommé to a gentle simmer, add the dumplings then cook over medium heat for 10 minutes or until just cooked through. Serve immediately, topped with the parsley.

Quick pea & ham soup with mint

Preparation time: 10 minutes
Cooking time: 10 minutes
Serves: 4

50 g (1¾ oz) butter
1 brown onion, finely chopped
500 g (1 lb 2 oz) frozen peas
375 ml (13 fl oz/1½ cups) good-quality chicken stock
375 ml (13 fl oz/1½ cups) water
¼ cup roughly chopped mint leaves, plus extra
   leaves, to serve
250 g (9 oz) leg ham, cut into strips

1 Melt the butter in a large saucepan over medium
heat. Add the onion and cook, stirring, for 5 minutes
or until soft.
2 Stir in the peas, stock and water and bring to the
boil over high heat. Reduce the heat and simmer,
covered, for 5 minutes.
3 Cool slightly then stir in the chopped mint and
transfer the soup in batches to a food processor or
blender and process until smooth. Return the soup
to the saucepan and reheat over medium heat. Stir in
the ham and season to taste with freshly ground black
pepper. Serve scattered with the extra mint leaves.

TIP: Taste the soup before seasoning with salt as the stock and ham will be quite salty.

Green tea, rice & salmon soup

Preparation time: 15 minutes
Cooking time: 20 minutes
Serves: 4

330 g (11½ oz/1½ cups) medium-grain white rice
560 ml (19¼ fl oz/2¼ cups) water
500 g (1 lb 2 oz) very fresh salmon fillets, skinned, pin-boned
300 g (10½ oz) silken tofu, drained, cut into 5 mm (¼ in) cubes
2 spring onions (scallions), trimmed, very thinly diagonally sliced
1.5 litres (52 fl oz/6 cups) freshly brewed, very hot Japanese green tea
fine strips of toasted nori, to serve
2 tablespoons toasted sesame seeds, to serve
wasabi and pickled ginger, to serve

1 Put the rice in a medium saucepan, add the water, cover the pan and bring to a simmer. Reduce the heat to low and cook for 12–15 minutes or until the water is absorbed. Remove from the heat and stand, covered, for 5 minutes or until the rice is tender.

2 Meanwhile, cut the salmon widthways into 5 mm (¼ in) thick slices.

3 Divide the rice among four bowls and scatter over the tofu and spring onion. Top with the salmon, then pour over the hot green tea. Serve immediately, topped with the nori strips and sesame seeds. Pass the wasabi and pickled ginger separately.

Basics

Clockwise from top left: pesto, spiced seeds,
gremolata, dukkah, crisp herbs

Gremolata

Preparation time: 3 minutes
Makes: ¼ cup

¼ cup very finely chopped flat-leaf (Italian) parsley
1 garlic clove, finely chopped
finely grated zest of 2 lemons

Combine the parsley, garlic and lemon zest in a small bowl.
Season well with salt.

TIP: Make the gremolata just before serving.

Crisp herbs

Preparation time: 3 minutes
Cooking time: 6 minutes
Serves: 2–4

160 ml (5¼ fl oz/⅔ cup) vegetable oil
¼ cup loosely packed herb leaves, such as sage,
     parsley, mint, basil or oregano (see tip)

Heat the vegetable oil in a small saucepan over medium
heat. Carefully add the herbs, six or seven leaves at a time
(even completely dry parsley and mint will spit slightly when
they first go in). Fry for 30–60 seconds or until the herbs
are crisp. Remove with a slotted spoon and drain on paper
towel. Repeat with the remaining herbs.

TIPS: Ensure that the herbs are completely dry as water will make the oil spit violently as you add the herbs. Patting them with paper towel works well.

You could make these up to 2 hours ahead of serving time.

Pesto

Preparation time: 5 minutes
Makes: ⅔ cup

> 55 g (2 oz/1¾ cups, loosely packed) basil
> 1 garlic clove, finely chopped
> 35 g (1¼ oz/⅓ cup) finely grated parmesan cheese
> 40 g (1½ oz/¼ cup) pine nuts
> 80 ml (2½ fl oz/⅓ cup) olive oil, plus 1 tablespoon extra

1 Place the basil, garlic, parmesan and pine nuts in a small food processor and pulse until roughly chopped. With the motor running, gradually add the olive oil and process until combined. Season to taste with salt and freshly ground black pepper.
2 Transfer to a small bowl and cover with the extra olive oil to preserve the colour of the pesto. Stir the olive oil through when ready to serve.

Variations

Rocket pesto: Replace the basil with 55 g (2 oz/1⅔ cups) wild rocket (arugula).
Mint pesto: Replace the basil with 55 g (2 oz/2¾ cups) mint leaves.

Dukkah

Preparation time: 2 minutes
Cooking time: 6 minutes
Makes: ⅔ cup

> 75 g (2¾ oz/½ cup) hazelnuts
> 2 tablespoons coriander seeds
> 1 tablespoon cumin seeds
> 2 tablespoons sesame seeds

TIP: Dukkah will keep in an airtight container in the fridge for up to 1 month. Bring to room temperature before serving.

1 Place the hazelnuts in a small frying pan over medium heat and toast for 4 minutes or until the skins darken, shaking the pan occasionally to ensure even cooking. Rub the warm hazelnuts in a tea towel (dish towel) to remove the skins.
2 Put the hazelnuts in a mortar with the coriander and cumin seeds and lightly crush with the pestle. Stir through the sesame seeds.
3 Transfer the dukkah to the frying pan over medium–low heat and gently toast, stirring occasionally, for 2 minutes or until aromatic. Transfer to a small bowl to cool.

Spiced seeds

Preparation time: 2 minutes
Cooking time: 4 minutes
Makes: 1 cup

1 teaspoon vegetable oil
10 g (¼ oz) butter, chopped
¼ teaspoon ground cumin
¼ teaspoon sweet paprika
75 g (2¾ oz/½ cup) pepitas (pumpkin seeds)
75 g (2¾ oz/½ cup) sunflower seeds

Place the vegetable oil, butter, cumin and paprika in a small saucepan over medium heat and cook for 30 seconds or until aromatic. Add the seeds and cook for 3 minutes, stirring occasionally, or until lightly toasted. Transfer to a baking tray lined with non-stick baking paper to cool.

TIP: Spiced seeds will keep in an airtight container in the fridge for up to 1 month. Bring to room temperature before serving.

Garlic bread

Preparation time: 10 minutes
Cooking time: 10 minutes
Serves: 4

4 small long rolls
100 g (3½ oz) butter, just softened
1 garlic clove, finely chopped
1 tablespoon finely chopped flat-leaf (Italian) parsley
3 teaspoons finely snipped chives
sea salt flakes

1 Preheat oven to 200°C (400°F/Gas 6). Make three diagonal cuts through the top of each roll but don't go all the way through. Combine the butter, garlic, herbs and a pinch of sea salt. Spread onto both sides of the cut bread.

2 Wrap each roll individually in foil, place on a baking tray and bake for 10 minutes or until crisp on the outside and the butter has melted. Serve immediately as whole rolls or broken into individual slices.

Variations

Sun-dried tomato & parmesan bread: Replace the garlic and herbs with 3 teaspoons finely chopped sun-dried tomatoes (not in oil) and 35 g (1¼ oz/⅓ cup) finely grated parmesan cheese.

Anchovy & rosemary bread: Replace the garlic and herbs with 2–3 finely chopped anchovy fillets and ¾ teaspoon very finely chopped rosemary.

Clockwise from top: chunky croutons, garlic bread, toasted cheesy soldiers, herbed sour cream spread

Herbed sour cream spread

Preparation time: 3 minutes
Makes: 125 g (4½ oz/½ cup)

>   125 g (4½ oz/½ cup) sour cream
>   1 tablespoon chopped flat-leaf (Italian) parsley
>   1 tablespoon chopped basil

Combine the sour cream, herbs and a pinch each
of salt and freshly ground black pepper in a bowl.

TIP: This spread is good
to use spooned on top of
soups just before serving
or spread onto toast
(instead of butter) to
accompany soups.

Chunky croutons

Preparation time: 5 minutes
Cooking time: 10 minutes
Makes: 2 cups

>   ½ loaf (about 350 g/12 oz) rustic bread (sourdough or ciabatta)
>   125 ml (4 fl oz/½ cup) olive oil
>   30 g (1 oz) butter, chopped
>   4 garlic cloves, lightly bruised

1 Remove the crust from the bread and tear the bread into rough 2–3 cm (¾–1¼ in) pieces.
(You will need about 4 cups loosely packed.)
2 Heat the olive oil, butter and garlic in a large frying pan over medium–low heat. (It should just
be gently bubbling not sizzling.) Add the croutons and use tongs to turn to coat in the oil. Cook
for 8–10 minutes, turning occasionally, until light golden and crisp. Remove with tongs and drain
on paper towel. Serve warm or at room temperature.

Toasted cheesy soldiers

Preparation time: 8 minutes
Cooking time: 3–4 minutes
Serves: 4

8 thick slices good-quality white bread
80 g (2¾ oz) butter, just softened
50 g (1¾ oz/½ cup, loosely packed) coarsely grated cheddar cheese
20 g (¾ oz) blue cheese (optional), crumbled

1 Preheat grill (broiler) to medium–high. Line a baking tray with foil.
2 Spread the bread slices with some of the butter. Top half of the slices with the cheddar cheese, then the blue cheese, if using. Top with the remaining bread slices to make four sandwiches, pressing down gently. Remove the crusts and then spread the outsides of each sandwich with the remaining butter. Place on the lined tray.
3 Place the sandwiches under preheated grill for 1–2 minutes or until toasted. Carefully remove the tray and use a spatula to turn the sandwiches. Return to the grill for 1–2 minutes or until toasted on the remaining slice. Slice each sandwich into three fingers and serve immediately.

Variations

Ricotta & parmesan toasts: Replace the cheddar and blue cheese with 80 g (2¾ oz/⅓ cup) firm, fresh ricotta cheese combined with 35 g (1¼ oz/⅓ cup) finely grated parmesan cheese.
Marinated feta & olive toasts: Replace the cheddar and blue cheese with 110 g (3¾ oz/¾ cup) crumbled, drained, marinated feta cheese combined with 1½ tablespoons chopped, pitted kalamata olives.

Index

First published in 2011 by Murdoch Books Pty Limited

Murdoch Books Australia
Pier 8/9
23 Hickson Road
Millers Point NSW 2000
Phone: +61 (0) 2 8220 2000
Fax: +61 (0) 2 8220 2558
www.murdochbooks.com.au

Murdoch Books UK Limited
Erico House, 6th Floor, 93–99 Upper
Richmond Road, Putney, London, SW15 2TG
Phone: +44 (0) 20 8785 5995
Fax: +44 (0) 20 8785 5985
www.murdochbooks.co.uk

Publisher: Kylie Walker
Food Development Editor: Anneka Manning
Project Editor: Laura Wilson
Editor: Melissa Penn
Design concept: Alex Frampton and Vivien Valk
Designers: Tania Gomes and R.T.J. Klinkhamer
Photographer: Michele Aboud
Stylist: Sarah de Nardi
Illustrator: Alex Frampton
Production: Renee Melbourne

Recipe development: Sonia Greig, Leanne Kitchen, Kirrily La Rosa, Lucy Nunes
Food preparation for photography: Lucy Lewis

National Library of Australia Cataloguing-in-Publication Data
Title: Soups.
ISBN: 978-1-74266-336-4 (pbk.)
Series: Make me.
Notes: Includes index.
Subjects: Soups.
Dewey Number: 641.813
A catalogue record for this book is available from the British Library.

Printed by 1010 Printing International Limited, China

OVEN GUIDE: You may find cooking times vary depending on the oven you are using.
For fan-forced ovens, as a general rule, set the oven temperature to 20°C (35°F) lower
than indicated in the recipe.

On cover: Carrot soup (page 104).